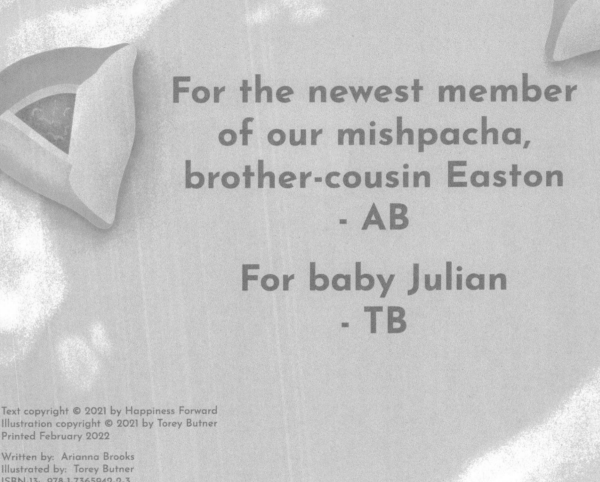

For the newest member
of our mishpacha,
brother-cousin Easton
- AB

For baby Julian
- TB

Text copyright © 2021 by Happiness Forward
Illustration copyright © 2021 by Torey Butner
Printed February 2022

Written by: Arianna Brooks
Illustrated by: Torey Butner
ISBN-13: 978-1-7365942-2-3
Library of Congress Control Number: 2021921307

Hungry for More by the Brooks/Butner Dream Team?
Visit: www.happinessforward.com

My Happy Hamentashen

written by
Arianna Brooks

illustrated by
Torey Butner

 Happiness Forward LLC

You are
my happy
hamentashen

(hah-muhn-tah-shuhn)

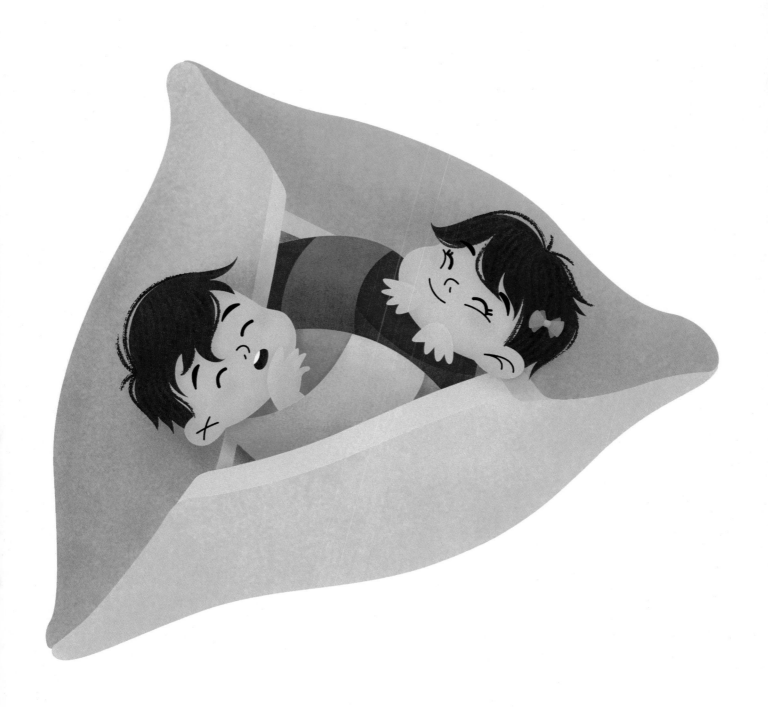

My rockin' rugelach

(rug-a-lach)

My
harmonious
challah

(haa-luh)

My sweet sufganiyot

(soof-gah-nee-YOHT)

My cozy kugel

(koo-gl)

My giggly
gefilte fish

(guh-fil-tuh fish)

My majestic matzah brei

(matzah-brigh)

and we will

always be

MISHPACHA

(family; meesh-pah-'HAH)

Yaya's Happy Hamentashen (Ruthie Cohen)

Ingredients:
- 1 stick butter
- 1/2 cup sugar
- 1 egg
- 3 Tablespoons milk
- 1 teaspoon vanilla
- 2 1/2 cups flour
- 1 teaspoon baking powder
- 1/4 teaspoon salt

Filling:
- apricot preserves
- cherry pie filling
- chocolate chips
- poppy seeds
- prune butter

Instructions (Ready in 2 hours):

Ingredients:
In a stand mixer, cream butter and sugar until fluffy.
Add egg, milk and vanilla. Blend in flour, baking powder, and salt.
Mix until combined.

On a floured surface, divide dough into two discs. Flatten each disc,
wrap tightly in plastic wrap and **refrigerate for an hour.**

Preheat oven to 350.

Remove dough from the refrigerator and allow it to come close to
room temperature. Flatten and roll out a disc on a floured surface to
about 1/4" thickness or less. Use the rim of a large drinking glass to cut out
circles in the dough. When you've made as many circles as possible, gather the
excess dough, re-roll and make more. Repeat with the second disc.
(Note: if you prefer smaller hamentashen use a little drinking glass and
adjust the filling amount accordingly.)

Place one teaspoon of your filling of choice in the center of each circle.
Form into a triangle: first fold the bottom of the circle over half of the
filling and press down to seal; then fold the sides over, while allowing the
filling to peek out; finally pinch dough together at the top and sides to seal.

Place hamentashen at wide intervals on a parchment lined cookie sheet.
(They will expand.) **Bake for 15 minutes until golden brown,**
Remove and cool on a cookie rack.

Made in the USA
Monee, IL
16 February 2022

91350386R00017